D1527677

# FORTUNE AND MEN'S EYES

# FORTUNE
# AND MEN'S EYES

New Poems with a Play

By
Josephine Preston Peabody

Boston and New York
Houghton Mifflin Company
*The Riverside Press Cambridge*

THIRD IMPRESSION

TO
MY MOTHER'S PRESENCE
AND
MY FATHER'S MEMORY ·

# CONTENTS

# CONTENTS

# FORTUNE AND MEN'S EYES

## A DRAMA IN ONE ACT

*" When in disgrace with Fortune and men's eyes"* . . .

Sonnet XXIX.

# CHARACTERS

WILLIAM HERBERT, *Son of the Earl of Pembroke*
SIMEON DYER, *A Puritan*
TOBIAS, *Host of " The Bear and The Angel "*
WAT BURROW, *A bear-ward*
DICKON, *A little boy, son to Tobias*
CHIFFIN, *A ballad-monger*
A PRENTICE

---

A PLAYER, *Master W. S. of the Lord Chamberlain's Company*

---

MISTRESS MARY FYTTON, *A maid-of-honor to Queen Elizabeth*
MISTRESS ANNE HUGHES, *Also of the Court*

TAVERNERS AND PRENTICES

*Time represented : An afternoon in the autumn of the year 1599*

# FORTUNE AND MEN'S EYES

SCENE : *Interior of " The Bear and the Angel,"
South London. At back, the centre entrance gives
on a short alley-walk which joins the street beyond at a right angle. To right and left of this
doorway, casements. Down, on the right, a door
opening upon the inn-garden ; a second door on the
right, up, leading to a tap-room. Opposite this, left,
a door leading into a buttery. Opposite the gar-
den-door, a large chimney-piece with a smouldering
wood-fire. A few seats ; a lantern (unlighted) in
a corner. In the foreground, to the right, a long
and narrow table with several mugs of ale upon it,
also a lute.*

*At one end of the table Wat Burrow is finishing
his ale and holding forth to the Prentice (who thrums
the lute) and a group of taverners, some smoking. At
the further end of the table Simeon Dyer observes all
with grave curiosity. Tobias and Dickon draw
near. General noise.*

PRENTICE (*singing*).
   *What do I give for the Pope and his riches !
   I's my ale and my Sunday breeches ;
   I's an old master, I's a young lass,
   And we'll eat green goose, come Martinmas !*

*Sing Rowdy Dowdy,*
*Look ye don't crowd me:*
*I's a good club,*
                              *— So let me pass!*

DICKON.    Again! again!

PRENTICE.                    *Sing Rowdy —*

WAT (*finishing his beer*).    Swallow it down.
Sling all such froth and follow me to the Bear!
They stay for me, lined up to see us pass
From end to end o' the alley.    Ho!    You doubt?
From Lambeth to the Bridge!

PRENTICES. }          { 'Tis so; ay.
TAVERNERS. }          { Come, follow!    Come.

WAT.                         Greg's stuck his ears
With nosegays, and his chain is wound about
Like any May-pole.    What?    I tell ye, boys,
Ye have seen no such bear, a Bear o' Bears,
Fit to bite off the prophet, in the show,
With seventy such boys!

(*Pulling Dickon's ear.*)    Bears, say you, bears?
Why, Rursus Major, as your scholars tell,
A royal bear, the greatest in his day,
The sport of Alexander, unto Nick —
Was a ewe-lamb, dyed black; no worse, no worse.
To-morrow come and see him with the dogs;
He'll not give way, — not he!

DICKON.                    To-morrow's Thursday!
To-morrow's Thursday!

PRENTICE.                        Will ye lead by here?

TOBIAS. Ay, that would be a sight. Wat,
man, this way!

WAT. Ho, would you squinch us? Why,
there be a press
O' gentry by this tide to measure Nick
And lay their wagers, at a blink of him,
Against to-morrow! Why, the stairs be full.
To-morrow you shall see the Bridge a-creak,
The river — dry with barges, — London gape,
Gape! While the Borough buzzes like a hive
With all their worships! Sirs, the fame o' Nick
Has so pluckt out the gentry by the sleeve,
'Tis said the Queen would see him.

TOBIAS. } { Ay, 'tis grand.
DICKON. } { O-oh, the Queen?

PRENTICE. How now? Thou art no man to
lead a bear,
Forgetting both his quality and hers!
Drink all; come, drink to her.

TOBIAS. Ay, now.

WAT. To her! —
And harkee, boy, this saying will serve you learn:
" The Queen, her high and glorious majesty! "

SIMEON (*gravely*). Long live the Queen!

WAT. Maker of golden laws
For baitings! She that cherishes the Borough
And shines upon our pastimes. By the mass!
Thank her for the crowd to-morrow. But for her,
We were a homesick handful of brave souls

That love the royal sport.    These mouthing
   players,
These hookers, would 'a' spoiled us of our beer —
 PRENTICE.    Lying by to catch the gentry at the
   stairs, —
All pressing to Bear Alley —
 WAT.        Run 'em in
At stage-plays and show-fooleries on the way.
Stage-plays, with their tart nonsense and their flags,
Their "Tamerlanes" and "Humors" and what
   not!
My life on't, there was not a man of us
But fared his Lent, by reason of their fatness,
And on a holiday ate not at all!
 TOBIAS (*solemnly*).    'Tis so; 'tis so.
 WAT.      But when she heard it told
How lean the sport was grown, she damns stage-
   plays
O' Thursday.    So : Nick gets his turn to
 growl!
 PRENTICE.    As well as any player.
(*With a dumb show of ranting among the taverners.*)
 WAT.     Players ? — Hang them!
I know 'em, I.    I've been with 'em. . . . I was
As sweet a gentlewoman in my voice
As any of your finches that sings small.
 TOBIAS.        'Twas high.
  (*Enter The Player, followed by Chiffin, the ballad-
   monger.    He is abstracted and weary.*)

WAT (*lingering at the table*).  I say, I've played.
    . . . There's not one man
Of all the gang — save one . . . Ay, there be one
I grant you, now !  . . . He used me in right sort ;
A man worth better trades.
    (*Seeing The Player.*)    — Lord love you, sir !
Why, this is you indeed.  'Tis a long day, sir,
Since I clapped eyes on you.  But even now
Your name was on my tongue as pat as ale !
You see me off.  We bait to-morrow, sir ;
Will you come see ?  Nick's fresh, and every soul
As hot to see the fight as 'twere to be —
Man Daniel, baited with the lions !
    TOBIAS.                    .                Sir,
'Tis high . . . 'tis high.
    WAT.              We show him in the street
With dogs and all, ay, now, if you will see.
    THE PLAYER.  Why, so I will.  A show and I
        not there?
Bear it out bravely, Wat.  High fortune, man !
Commend me to thy bear.
    (*Drinks and passes him the cup.*)
    WAT.                  Lord love you, sir !
'Twas ever so you gave a man godspeed. . . .
And yet your spirits flag ; you look but palely.
I'll take your kindness, thank ye.
    (*Turning away.*)              In good time !
Come after me and Nick, now.  Follow all ;
Come boys, come, pack !

*(Exit Wat, still descanting.  Exeunt most of*
*the taverners, with the Prentice.  Simeon*
*Dyer draws near The Player, regarding him*
*gravely.  Chiffin sells ballads to those who go*
*out.  Dickon is about to follow them, when*
*Tobias stops him.)*

TOBIAS.          What ?  Not so fast, you there ;
Who gave you holiday ?    Bide by the inn ;
Tend on our gentry.        *(Exit after the crowd.)*

CHIFFIN.              Ballads, gentlemen ?
Ballads, new ballads ?

SIMEON *(to The Player)*.   With your pardon,
    sir,
I am gratified to note your abstinence
From this deplorable fond merriment
Of baiting of a bear.

THE PLAYER.          Your friendship then
Takes pleasure in the heaviness of my legs.
But I am weary I would see the bear.
Nay, rest you happy ; malt shall comfort us.

SIMEON.    You do mistake me.    I am —

CHIFFIN.                          Ballad, sir ?
" How a Young Spark would Woo a Tanner's Wife,
And She Sings Sweet in Turn."

SIMEON *(indignantly)*.        Abandoned poet !

CHIFFIN *(indignantly)*.    I'm no such thing !
    An honest ballad, sir,
No poetry at all.

THE PLAYER.    Good, sell thy wares.

CHIFFIN.   "A Ballad of a Virtuous Country-
    Maid
Forswears the Follies of the Flaunting Town" —
And tends her geese all day, and weds a vicar.
    SIMEON.   A godlier tale, in sooth.   But speak,
    my man ;
If she be virtuous, and the tale a true one,
Can she not do't in prose?
    THE PLAYER.                Beseech her, man.
'Tis scandal she should use a measure so.
For no more sin than dealing out false measure
Was Dame Sapphira slain.
    SIMEON.                You are with me, sir;
Although methinks you do mistake the sense
O' that you have read. . . . This jigging, jog-trot
    rime,
This ring-me-round, debaseth mind and matter,
To make the reason giddy —
    CHIFFIN (to The Player).        Ballad, sir?
"Hear All!"   A fine brave ballad of a Fish
Just caught off Dover ; nay, a one-eyed fish,
With teeth in double rows.
    THE PLAYER.                Nay, nay, go to.
    CHIFFIN.   "My Fortune's Folly," then ;   or
    "The True Tale
Of an Angry Gull ; " or "Cherries Like Me
    Best."
"Black Sheep, or How a Cut-Purse Robbed His
    Mother ; "

"The Prentice and the Dell!" . . . "Plays Play
    not Fair,"
Or how a *gentlewoman's* heart was took
By a player that was king in a stage-play. . . .
"The Merry Salutation," "How a Spark
Would Woo a Tanner's Wife!"   "The Direful
    Fish" —
Cock's passion, sir! not buy a cleanly ballad
Of the great fish, late ta'en off Dover coast,
Having two heads and teeth in double rows. . . .
Salt fish catched in fresh water? . . .
                                    'Od's my life!
What if or salt or fresh?   A prodigy!
A ballad like "Hear All!"   And me and
    mine,
Five children and a wife would bait the devil,
May lap the water out o' Lambeth Marsh
Before he'll buy a ballad.   My poor wife,
That lies a-weeping for a tansy-cake!
Body o' me, shall I scent ale again?
    THE PLAYER.   Why, here's persuasion; logic,
    arguments.
Nay, not the ballad.   Read for thine own joy.
I doubt not but it stretches, honest length,
From Maid Lane to the Bridge and so across.
But for thy length of thirst —
        (*Giving him a coin.*)        That touches near.
    CHIFFIN (*apart*).   A vagrom player, would not
    buy a tale

O' the Great Fish with the twy rows o' teeth!
Learn you to read!                    (*Exit.*)
   SIMEON.   Thou seemest, sir, from that I have
      overheard,
A man, as one should grant, beyond thy calling. . . .
I would I might assure thee of the way,
To urge thee quit this painted infamy.
There may be time, seeing thou art still young,
To pluck thee from the burning.   How are ye
      'stroyed,
Ye foolish grasshoppers!   Cut off, forgotten,
When moth and rust corrupt your flaunting
      shows,
The Earth shall have no memory of your name!
   DICKON.   Pray you, what's yours?
   SIMEON.               I am called Simeon Dyer.
   (*There is the sudden uproar of a crowd in the
      distance.   It continues at intervals for some
      time.*)

PRENTICES. {
   Hey, lads?
   Some noise beyond: Come, cud-
      gels, come!
   Come on, come on, I'm for it.
}

   (*Exeunt all but The Player, Simeon, and
      Dickon.*)
   SIMEON.   Something untoward, without: or is
      it rather
The tumult of some uproar incident
To this . . . vicinity?

THE PLAYER.          It is an uproar
Most incident to bears.
          DICKON.                    I would I knew!
          THE PLAYER (*holding him off at arm's length*).
Hey, boy?   We would have tidings of the bear:
Go thou, I'll be thy surety.   Mark him well.
Omit no fact; I would have all of it:
What manner o' bear he is, — how bears him-
          self;
Number and pattern of ears, and eyes what hue;
His voice and fashion o' coat.   Nay, come not
          back,
Till thou hast all.   Skip, sirrah!   (*Exit Dickon.*)
          SIMEON.                    Think, fair sir.
Take this new word of mine to be a seed
Of thought in that neglected garden plot,
Thy mind, thy worthier part.   But think!
          THE PLAYER.                    Why, so;
Thou hast some right, friend; now and then it
          serves.
Sometimes I have thought, and even now some-
          times,
. . . I think.
          SIMEON (*benevolently*).   Heaven ripen thought
          unto an harvest!                    (*Exit.*)
          (*The Player rises, stretches his arms, and paces
          the floor, wearily.*)
          THE PLAYER (*alone*).   Some quiet now. . . .
          Why should I thirst for it

As if my thoughts were noble company ?
Alone with the one man of all living men
I have least cause to honor. . . .
                              I'm no lover,
That seek to be alone ! . . . She is too false —
At last, to keep a spaniel's loyalty.
I do believe it.   And by my own soul,
She shall not have me, what remains of me
That may be beaten back into the ranks.
I will not look upon her. . . . Bitter Sweet.
This fever that torments me day by day —
Call it not love — this servitude, this spell
That haunts me like a sick man's fantasy,
With pleading of her eyes, her voice, her eyes —
It shall not have me.   I am too much stained :
But, God or no God, yet I do not live
And have to bear my own soul company,
To have it stoop so low.   She looks on Herbert.
Oh, I have seen.   But he, — he must withstand.
He knows that I have suffered, — suffer still —
Although I love her not.   Her ways, her ways —
It is her ways that eat into the heart
With beauty more than Beauty; and her voice
That silvers o'er the meaning of her speech
Like moonshine on black waters.   Ah, un-
     coil ! . . .
He's the sure morning after this dark dream ;
Clear daylight and west wind of a lad's love;
With all his golden pride, for my dull hours,

Still climbing sunward! Sink all loves in him!
And cleanse me of this cursèd, fell distrust
That marks the pestilence. . . .

                 '*Fair, kind, and true.*'
Lad, lad. How could I turn from friendliness
To worship such false gods? —
There cannot thrive a greater love than this,
'*Fair, kind, and true.*' And yet, if She were true
To me, though false to all things else; — one
     truth,
So one truth lived —. One truth! O beggared
     soul,
— Foul Lazarus, so starved it can make shift
To feed on crumbs of honor! — Am I this?

    (*Enter Anne Hughes. She has been running
         in evident terror, and stands against the door
         looking about her.*)

  ANNE. Are you the inn-keeper?
(*The Player turns and bows courteously.*)

                  Nay, sir, your pardon.
I saw you not . . . And yet your face, methinks,
But — yes, I'm sure. . . .

               But where's the inn-keeper?
I know not where I am, nor where to go.

  THE PLAYER. Madam, it is my fortune that
     I may
Procure you service. (*Going towards the door.*)
    (*The uproar sounds nearer.*)

ANNE.                        Nay! what if the
    bear —
THE PLAYER.   The bear?
ANNE.   The door!   The bear is broken loose.
Did you not hear?   I scarce could make my way
Through that rank crowd, in search of some safe
    place.
You smile, sir!   But you had not seen the bear, —
Nor I, this morning.   Pray you, hear me out, —
For surely you are gentler than the place.
I came . . . I came by water . . . to the Garden,
Alone, . . . from bravery, to see the show
And tell of it hereafter at the Court!
There's one of us makes count of all such 'scapes
('Tis Mistress Fytton).   She will ever tell
The sport it is to see the people's games
Among themselves, — to go *incognita*
And take all as it is not for the Queen,
Gallants and rabble!   But by Banbury Cross,
I am of tamer mettle! — All alone,
Among ten thousand noisy watermen;
And then the foul ways leading from the Stair;
And then . . . no friends I knew, nay, not a
    face.
And my dear nose beset, and my pomander
Lost in the rout, — or else a cut-purse had it:
And then the bear breaks loose!   Oh, 'tis a day
Full of vexations, nay, and dangers too.
I would I had been slower to outdo

The pranks of Mary Fytton. . . . You know
    her, sir?
    THE PLAYER.   If one of my plain calling may
        be said
To know a maid-of-honor.   (*More lightly*.)   And
    yet more :
My heart has cause to know the lady's face.
    ANNE (*blankly*).   Why, so it is. . . . Is't not
        a marvel, sir,
The way she hath?   Truly, her voice is good. . . .
And yet, — but oh, she charms; I hear it said.
A winsome gentlewoman, of a wit, too.
We are great fellows; she tells me all she does ;
And, sooth, I listen till my ears be like
To grow for wonder.   Whence my 'scape, to-day!
Oh, she hath daring for the pastimes here ;
I would — change looks with her, to have her
    spirit !
Indeed, they say she charms Some one, by this.
    THE PLAYER.   Some one. . . .
    ANNE.                            Hast heard?
        Why sure my Lord of Herbert,
Ay, Pembroke's son.   But there I doubt, — I
    doubt.
He is an eagle will not stoop for less
Than kingly prey.   No bird-lime takes him.
    THE PLAYER.                            Herbert. . . .
He hath shown many favors to us players.
    ANNE.   Ah, now I have you !

THE PLAYER.            Surely, gracious madam;
My duty; . . . what besides?
    ANNE.                This face of yours.
'Twas in some play, belike.  (*Apart.*) . . .
        I took him for
A man it should advantage me to know!
And he's a proper man enough. . . . Ay me!
        (*When she speaks to him again it is with en-
        couraging condescension.*)
Surely you've been at Whitehall, Master Player?
    THE PLAYER (*bowing*).  So.
    ANNE.            And how oft?  And when?
    THE PLAYER.            Last Christmas tide;
And Twelfth Day eve, perchance.  Your memory
Freshens a dusty past. . . . The hubbub's over.
Shall I look forth and find some trusty boy
To attend you to the river?
    ANNE.                I thank you, sir.
        (*He goes to the door and steps out into the
        alley, looking up and down.  The noise in the
        distance springs up again.*)
    (*Apart.*)  'Tis not past sufferance.  Marry, I
        could stay
Some moments longer, till the streets be safe.
Sir, sir!
    THE PLAYER (*returning*).  Command me,
        madam.
    ANNE.        I will wait
A little longer, lest I meet once more

That ruffian mob or any of the dogs.
These sports are better seen from balconies.

THE PLAYER.   Will you step hither?   There's
an arbored walk

Sheltered and safe.   Should they come by again,
You may see all, an't like you, and be hid.

ANNE.   A garden there?   Come, you shall
show it me.

(*They go out into the garden on the right, leaving the door shut.   Immediately enter, in
great haste, Mary Fytton and William
Herbert, followed by Dickon, who looks about
and, seeing no one, goes to setting things in
order.*)

MARY.   Quick, quick! . . . She must have
seen me.   Those big eyes,

How could they miss me, peering as she was
For some familiar face?   She would have known,
Even before my mask was jostled off
In that wild rabble . . . bears and bearish men.

HERBERT.   Why would you have me bring you?

MARY.                          Why?   Ah, why!

Sooth, once I had a reason:   now 'tis lost, —
Lost!   Lost!   Call out the bell-man.

DICKON (*seriously*).                Shall I so?

HERBERT.   Nay, nay; that were a merriment
indeed,

To   cry   us   through   the   streets!    (*To   Mary.*)
You riddling charm.

MARY.    A riddle, yet?    You almost love me,
    then.
HERBERT.    Almost?
MARY.            Because you cannot understand.
Alas, when all's unriddled, the charm goes.
HERBERT.    Come, you're not melancholy?
MARY.                        Nay, are you?
But should Nan Hughes have seen us, and spoiled
    all —
HERBERT.    How could she so?
MARY.            I know not . . . yet I know
If she had met us, she could steal To-day,
Golden To-day.
HERBERT.        A kiss; and so forget her.
MARY.    Hush, hush, — the tavern-boy there.
  (*To Dickon.*)                Tell me, boy, —
  (*To Herbert.*)    Some errand, now; a roc's egg!
    Strike thy wit.
HERBERT.    What is't you miss?    Why, so.
    The lady's lost
A very curious reason, wrought about
With diverse broidery.
MARY.                Nay, 'twas a mask.
HERBERT.    A mask, arch-wit?    Why will you
    mock yourself
And all your fine deceits?    Your mask, your rea-
    son,
Your reason with a mask!
MARY.                    You are too merry.

(*To Dickon.*)    A mask it is, and muffler finely
        wrought
With little amber points all hung like bells.
I lost it as I came, somewhere. . . .
        HERBERT.                            Somewhere
Between the Paris Gardens and the Bridge.
        MARY.    Or below Bridge — or haply  in  the
            Thames !
        HERBERT.    No matter where, so you do bring
            it back.
Fly, Mercury !   Here's feathers for thy heels.
                                    (*Giving coin.*)
        MARY (*aside*).    Weights, weights !
                                    (*Exit  Dickon.*)
        (*Herbert  looks about  him, opens  the  door of the
            tap-room, grows  troubled.    She  watches  him
            with  dissatisfaction, seeming to  warm  her feet
            by the fire meanwhile.*)
        HERBERT (*apart*).    I  know  this  place.   We
            used to come
Together, he and I . . .
        MARY (*apart*).            Forgot again.
O the capricious tides, the hateful calms,
And the too eager ship that would be gone
Adventuring against uncertain winds,
For some new, utmost sight of Happy Isles !
Becalmed, — becalmed  . . .  But I will break this
            calm.
        (*She  sees  the lute on the table, crosses and takes*

*it up, running her fingers over the strings*
*very softly.   She sits.*)

HERBERT.   Ah, mermaid, is it you?

MARY.                        Did you sail far?

HERBERT.   Not I; no, sooth.   (*Crossing to her.*)
                      Mermaid, I would not think.
But you ---

MARY.     I think not.   I remember nothing.
There's nothing in the world but you and me;
All else is dust.   Thou shalt not question me;
Or if, — but as a sphinx in woman-shape :
And when thou fail'st at answer, I shall turn,
And rend thy heart and cast thee from the cliff.
      (*She leans her head back against him, and he*
      *kisses her.*)
So perish all who guess not what I am! . . .
Oh, but I know you : you are April-Days.
Nothing is sure, but all is beautiful !
      (*She runs her fingers up the strings, one by one,*
      *and listens, speaking to the lute.*)
Is it not so?   Come, answer.   Is it true?
Speak, sweeting, since I love thee best of late,
And have forsook my virginals for thee.
*All's beautiful indeed and all unsure?*
" *Ay* " . . . (Did you hear?)   *He's fair and faith-*
      *less?*   " *Ay.*"   (*Speaking with the lute.*)

HERBERT.   Poor oracle, with only one reply ! —
Wherein 'tis unlike thee.

MARY.                    *Can he love aught*

*So well as his own image in the brook,*
*Having once seen it?*

    HERBERT.           Ay!

    MARY.             The lute saith " *No*." . . .

O dullard! Here were tidings, would you mark.
What said I? *Oracle, can he love aught*
*So dear as his own image in the brook,*
*Having once looked?* . . . No, truly.

    (*With sudden abandon.*)         Nor can I!

    HERBERT. O leave this game of words, you
        thousand-tongued.

Sing, sing to me. So shall I be all yours
Forever; — or at least till you be mute! . . .
I used to wonder he should be thy slave:
I wonder now no more. Your ways are wonders;
You have a charm to make a man forget
His past and yours, and everything but you.

    MARY (*speaking*).

      " *When daisies pied and violets blue*
           *And lady-smocks all silver-white* " —

How now?

    HERBERT. " How now ? " That song . . .
        thou wilt sing that?

    MARY. Marry, what mars the song?

    HERBERT.               Have you forgot
Who made it?

    MARY.       Soft, what idleness! So fine?
So rude? And bid me sing! You get but silence;
Or, if I sing, — beshrew me, it shall be

A dole of song, a little starveling breath
As near to silence as a song can be.
>    (*She sings under-breath, fantastically.*)
>            *Say how many kisses be*
>            *Lent and lost twixt you and me?*
>            *' Can I tell when they begun?'*
>            *Nay, but this were prodigal:*
>            *Let us learn to count withal.*
>            *Since no ending is to spending,*
>            *Sum our riches, one by one.*
>            *' You shall keep the reckoning,*
>            *Count each kiss while I do sing.'*

HERBERT.   Oh, not these little wounds.   You
>    vex my heart;
Heal it again with singing, — come, sweet, come.
Into the garden !   None shall trouble us.
This place has memories and conscience too :
Drown all, my mermaid.   Wind them in your
>    hair
And drown them, drown them all.
>    (*He swings open the garden-door for her.   At
>    the same moment Anne's voice is heard ap-
>    proaching.*)

ANNE (*without*).            Some music there?

HERBERT.   Perdition !   Quick, — behind me,
>    love.
>    (*Swinging the door shut again, and looking
>    through the crack.*)

MARY.   'Tis she —

Nan Hughes, 'tis she!   How came she here ?  By
    heaven,
She crosses us to-day.   Nan Hughes lights here
In a Bank tavern!   Nay, I'll not be seen.
Sooner or later it must mean the wreck
Of both . . .  should the Queen know.

HERBERT.                      The spite of chance !
She talks with some one in the arbor there
Whose face I see not.   Come, here's doors at
    least.

> (*They cross hastily.  Mary opens the door on
> the left and looks within.*)

MARY.   Too thick. . . . I shall be penned.
    But guard you this
And tell me when they're gone.   Stay, stay ; —
    mend all.
If she have seen me, — swear it was not I.
Heaven speed her home, with her new body-guard !

> (*Exit, closing door.  Herbert looks out into the
> garden.*)

HERBERT.   By all accursèd chances, — none but
    he !

> (*Retires up to stand beside the door, looking out
> of casement.  Reënter from the garden,
> Anne, followed by The Player.*)

ANNE.   No, 'twas some magic in my ears, I
    think.
There's no one here.   (*Seeing Herbert.*)

                      But yes, there's some one here : —

The innkeeper.   Are you —
                    Saint Catherine's bones!
My Lord of Herbert.   Sir, you could not look
More opportune.   But for this gentleman —
 HERBERT (*bowing*).   My friend, this long time
  since, —
 ANNE.  Marry, your friend?
 THE PLAYER (*regarding Herbert searchingly*).
This long time since.
 ANNE.   Nay, is it so, indeed?
 (*To Herbert.*)   My day's fulfilled of blunders!
  O sweet sir,
How can I tell you?   But I'll tell you all
If you'll but bear me escort from this place
Where none of us belongs.   Yours is the first
Familiar face I've seen this afternoon!
 HERBERT (*apart*).   A sweet assurance.
  (*Aloud.*)  But you seek . . . you need
Some rest — some cheer, some — Will you step
  within?   (*Indicating tap-room.*)
The tavern is deserted, but —
 ANNE.   Not here!
I've been here quite an hour.   Come, citywards,
To Whitehall!   I have had enough of bears
To quench my longing till next Whitsuntide.
Down to the river, pray you.
 HERBERT.   Sooth, at once?
 ANNE.   At once, at once.
 (*To The Player.*)  I crave your pardon, sir,

For sundering your friendships.   I've heard say
A woman always comes between two men
To their confusion.   You shall drink amends
Some other day.   I must be safely home.

    THE PLAYER (*reassured by Herbert's reluctance
      to go*).

It joys me that your trials have found an end ;
And for the rest, I wish you prosperous voyage ;
Which needs not, with such halcyon weather
    toward.

    HERBERT (*apart*).    It cuts : and yet he
    knows not.   Can it pass ?
    (*To him.*)   Let us meet soon.   I have — I
    know not what

To say — nay, no import ; but chance has parted
Our several ways too long.   To leave you thus,
Without a word —

    ANNE.            You are in haste, my lord !
By the true faith, here are two friends indeed !
Two lovers crossed : and I, — 'tis I that bar them.
Pray tarry, sir.   I doubt not I may light
Upon some link-boy to attend me home
Or else a drunken prentice with a club,
Or that patched keeper strolling from the Garden
With all his dogs along ; or failing them,
A pony with a monkey on his back,
Or, failing that, a bear !   Some escort, sure,
Such as the Borough offers !   I shall look
Part of a pageant from the Lady Fair,

And boast for three full moons, " Such sights I
    saw ! "
Truly, 'tis new to me : but I doubt not
I shall trick out a mind for strange adventure,
As high as — Mistress Fytton !

HERBERT.                  Say no more,
Dear lady ! I entreat you pardon me
The lameness of my wit. I'm stark adream ;
You lighted here so suddenly, unlooked for
Vision in Bankside. . . . Let me hasten you,
Now that I see I dream not. It grows late.

ANNE. And can you grant me such a length
    of time ?

HERBERT. Length ? Say Illusion ! Time ?
    Alas, 'twill be
Only a poor half-hour, (*loudly*) a poor half-hour !
    (*Apart.*) Did she hear that, I wonder ?

THE PLAYER (*bowing over Anne's hand*). Not
    so, madam ;
A little gold of largess, fallen to me
By chance.

HERBERT (*to him*). A word with you —
    (*Apart.*)            O, I am gagged !

ANNE (*to The Player*). You go with us, sir ?
    (*He moves towards door with them.*)

THE PLAYER.          No, I do but play
Your inn-keeper.

HERBERT (*apart, despairingly*). The eagle is
    gone blind.

> (*Exeunt, leaving doors open. They are seen to go down the walk together. At the street they pause, The Player, bowing slowly, then turning back towards the inn; Anne holding Herbert's arm. Within, the door on the left opens slightly, then Mary appears.*)

MARY.    'Tis true.    My ears caught silence, if no more.

They're gone. . . .

> (*She comes out of her hiding-place and opens the left-hand casement to see Anne disappearing with Herbert.*)

She takes him with her!   He'll return?

Gone, gone, without a word; and I was caged, —

And deaf as well.    O, spite of everything!

She's so unlike. . . .    How long shall I be here

To  wait  and  wonder?    He with her — with her!

> (*The Player, having come slowly back to the door, hears her voice. Mary darts towards the entrance to look after Herbert and Anne. She sees him and recoils. She falls back step by step, while he stands holding the door-posts with his hands, impassive.*)

You! . . .

THE  PLAYER.    Yes. . . . (*After  a  pause.*)

And you.

MARY.                        Do you not ask me why

I'm here?

THE PLAYER. I am not wont to shun the
    truth:
But yet I think the reason you could give
Were too uncomely.
    MARY.            Nay; —
    THE PLAYER.                    If it were truth;
If it were truth! Although that likelihood
Scarce threatens.
    MARY.        So. Condemned without a trial.
    THE PLAYER. O, speak the lie now. Let
        there be no chance
For my unsightly love, bound head and foot,
Stark, full of wounds and horrible, — to find
Escape from out its charnel-house; to rise
Unwelcome before eyes that had forgot,
And say it died not truly. It should die.
Play no imposture: leave it, — it is dead.
I have been weak in that I tried to pour
The wine through plague-struck veins. It came
        to life
Over and over, drew sharp breath again
In torture such as't may be to be born,
If a poor babe could tell. Over and over,
I tell you, it has suffered resurrection,
Cheating its pain with hope, only to die
Over and over; — die more deaths than men
The meanest, most forlorn, are made to die
By tyranny or nature. . . . Now I see all
Clear. And I say, it shall not rise again.

I am as safe from you as I were dead.
I know you.

MARY.        Herbert —

THE PLAYER.        Do not touch his name.
Leave that; I saw.

MARY.        You saw? Nay, what?

THE PLAYER.        The whole
Clear story. Not at first. While you were hid,
I took some comfort, drop by drop, and minute
By minute. (Dullard!) Yet there was a maze
Of circumstance that showed even then to me
Perplext and strange. You here unravel it.
All's clear: you are the clew.    (*Turning away.*)

MARY (*going to the casement.*)

    (*Apart.*)        Caged, caged!
Does he know all? Why were those walls so
    dense?

(*To him.*) Nan Hughes hath seized the time to
    tune your mind
To some light gossip. Say, how came she here?

THE PLAYER. All emulation, thinking **to**
    match you
In high adventure: — liked it not, poor lady!
And is gone home, attended.

    (*Reënter Dickon.*)

DICKON (*to Mary*).        They be lost! —
Thy mask and muffler; — 'tis no help to search.
Some hooker would 'a' swallowed 'em, be sure,
As the whale swallows Jonas, in the show.

MARY.   'Tis nought: I care not.

DICKON (*looking at the fire*).   Hey, it wants a
   log.

   (*While he mends the fire, humming, The Player
      stands taking thought.  Mary speaks apart,
      going to casement again to look out.*)

MARY (*apart*).   I will have what he knows.
   To cast me off: —

Not thus, not thus.   Peace, I can blind him yet,
Or he'll despise me.   Nay, I will not be
Thrust out at door like this.   I will not go
But by mine own free will.   There is no power
Can say what he might do to ruin us,
To win Will Herbert from me, — almost mine,
And I all his, all his — O April-Days ! —
Well, friendship against love ?   I know who wins.
He is grown dread. . . .   But yet he is a man.

                (*Exit Dickon into tap-room.*)

(*To The Player, suavely.*)   Well, headsman ?

            (*He does not turn.*)

        Mind your office: I am judged.
Guilty, was it not so ? . . .   What is to do,
Do quickly. . . .   Do you wait for some reprieve ?
Guilty, you said.   Nay, do you turn your face
To give me some small leeway of escape ?
And yet, I will not go . . .

        (*Coming down slowly.*)

            Well, headsman ? . . .
You ask not why I came here, Clouded Brow,

Will you not ask me why I stay? No word?
O blind, come lead the blind! For I, I too
Lack sight and every sense to linger here
And make me an intruder where I once
Was welcome, oh most welcome, as I dreamed.
Look on me, then. I do confess, I have
Too often preened my feathers in the sun
And thought to rule a little, by my wit.
I have been spendthrift with men's offerings
To use them like a nosegay, — tear apart,
Petal by petal, leaf by leaf, until
I found the heart all bare, the curious heart
I longed to see for once, and cast away.
And so, at first, with you. . . . Ah, now I think
You're wise. There's nought so fair, so . . .
    curious,
So precious-rare to find as honesty.
'Twas all a child's play then, a counting-off
Of petals. Now I know. . . . But ask me why
I come unheralded, and in a mist
Of circumstance and strangeness. Listen, love;
Well then, dead love, if you will have it so.
I have been cunning, cruel, — what you will:
And yet the days of late have seemed too long
Even for summer! Something called me here.
And so I flung my pride away and came,
A very woman for my foolishness,
To say once more, — to say . . .
   The Player.         Nay, I'll not ask.

What lacks ?    I need no more, you have done well.
'Tis rare.    There is no man I ever saw
But you could school him.    Women should be
      players.
You are sovran in the art : feigning and truth
Are so commingled in you.    Sure, to you
Nature's a simpleton hath never seen
Her own face in the well.    Is there aught else ?
To ask of my poor calling ?

MARY.                        I deserved it
In other days.    Hear how I can be meek.
I am come back, a foot-worn runaway,
Like any braggart boy.    Let me sit down
And take Love's horn-book in my hands again
And learn from the beginning ; — by the rod,
If you will scourge me, love.    Come, come, for-
      give.
I am not wont to sue : and yet to-day
I am your suppliant, I am your servant,
Your link-boy, ay, your minstrel : ay, — wilt hear ?
      (*Takes up the lute, and gives a last look out
        of the casement.*)
The tumult in the streets is all apart
With the discordant past.    The hour that is
Shall be the only thing in all the world.
      (*Apart.*)    I will be safe.    He'll not win Her-
      bert from me !
      (*Crossing to him.*)
Will you have music, good my lord ?

THE PLAYER (*catching the lute from her*).   Not
    that,
Not that!   By heaven, you shall not. . . .
    Nevermore.
    MARY.   So . . . But you speak at last.   You
    are, forsooth,
A man : and you shall use me as my due ; —
A woman, not the wind about your ears ;
A woman whom you loved.
    THE PLAYER (*half-apart, still holding the lute*).
                        Why were you not
That beauty that you seemed? . . . But had you
    been,
'Tis true, you would have had no word for me, —
No looks of love !
    MARY.          The man reproaches me?
    THE PLAYER.   Not I — not I. . . . Will
    Herbert, what am I
To lay this broken trust to you, — to you,
Young, free, and tempted : April on his way,
Whom all hands reach for, and this woman here
Had set her heart upon !
    MARY               What fantasy !
Surely he must have been from town of late,
To see the gude-folks !   And how fare they, sir ?
Reverend yeoman, say, how thrive the sheep ?
What did the harvest yield you ? — Did you count
The cabbage heads ? and find how like . . .
    nay,  nay !

But our gude-wife, did she bid in the neighbors
To prove them that her husband was no myth?
Some Puritan preacher, nay, some journeyman,
To make you sup the sweeter with long prayers?
This were a rare conversion, by my soul!
From sonnets unto sermons: — eminent!

   THE PLAYER.   Oh, yes, your scorn bites truly:
     sermons next.
There is so much to say. But it must be
     learned,
And I require hard schooling, dream too much
On what I would men were, — but women most.
I need the cudgel of the task-master
To make me con the truth. Yes, blind, you called
     me,
And 'tis my shame I bandaged mine own eyes
And held them dark. Now, by the grace of
     God,
Or haply because the devil tries too far,
I tear the blindfold off, and I see all.
I see you as you are; and in your heart
The secret love sprung up for one I loved,
A reckless boy who has trodden on my soul —
But that's a thing apart, concerns not you.
I know that you will stake your heaven and earth
To fool me, — fool us both.

   MARY (*with idle interest*).   Why were you not
So stern a long time since? You're not so wise
As I have heard them say.

THE PLAYER (*standing by the chimney*).   Wise ?
    Oh, not I.
Who was so witless as to call me wise ?
Sure he had never bade me a good-day
And seen me take the cheer. . . .

                         I was your fool
Too long. . . . I am no longer anything.
Speak : what are you ?
    MARY (*after a pause*).   The foolishest of
    women :
A heart that should have been adventurer
On the high seas ; a seeker in new lands,
To dare all and to lose.   But I was made
A woman.

            Oh, you see ! — could you see all.
What if I say . . . the truth is not so far,
               (*watching him*)
Yet farther than you dream.   If I confess . . .
He charmed my fancy . . . for the moment, — ay
The shine of his fortunes too, the very name
Of Pembroke ? . . . Dear my judge, — ah, clouded
    brow
And darkened fortune, be not black to me !
I'd try for my escape ; the window's wide,
No one forbids, and yet I stay — I stay.

   .     .     .     .     .     .     .

Oh, I was niggard, once, unkind — I know,
Untrusty : loved, unloved you, day by day :
A little and a little, — why, I knew not,

And more, and wondered why; — then not at all :
Drank up the dew from out your very heart,
Like the extortionate sun, to leave you parched
Till, with as little grace, I flung all back
In gusts of angry rain !  I have been cruel.
But the spell works; yea, love, the spell, the spell
Fed by your fasting, by your subtlety
Past all men's knowledge. . . . There is something
    rare
About you that I long to flee and cannot : —
Some mastery . . . that's more my will than I.
    (*She laughs softly.  He listens, looking straight
    ahead, not at her, immobile, but suffering
    evidently.  She watches his face and speaks
    with greater intensity.  Here she crosses
    nearer and falls on her knees.*)
Ah, look : you shall believe, you shall believe.
Will you put by your Music ?  Was I that ?
Your Music, — very Music ? . . . Listen, then,
Turn not so blank a face.  Thou hast my love.
I'll tell thee so till thought itself shall tire
And fall a-dreaming like a weary child, . . .
Only to dream of you, and in its sleep
To murmur You. . . . Ah, look at me, love,
    lord . . .
Whom queens would honor.  Read these eyes you
    praised,
That pitied, once, — that sue for pity now.
But look !  You shall not turn from me —

THE PLAYER.                           Eyes, eyes ! —
The darkness hides so much.

MARY.                         He'll not believe. . . .
What can I do?   What more, — what more, you
     . . . man?
I bruise my heart here, at an iron gate. . . .
     (*She regards him half gloomily without rising.*)
Yet there is one thing more. . . . You'll take me,
     now? —
My meaning. . . . You were right.   For once I
     say it.
There is a glory of discovery (*ironically*)
To the black heart . . . because it may be
     known
But once, — but once. . . .
                              I wonder men will hide
Their motives all so close.   If they could guess, —
It is so new to feel the open day
Look in on all one's hidings, at the end.
So. . . . You were right.   The first was all
     a lie :
A lie, and for a purpose . . . . . .
Now, — (*she rises and stands off, regarding him
     abruptly*),
And why, I know not, — but 'tis true, at last,
I do believe . . . I love you.
                              Look at me !
     (*He stands by the fireside against the chimney-
     piece.   She crosses to him with passionate*

*appeal, holding out her arms.    He turns his
eyes and looks at her with a rigid scrutiny.
She endures it for a second, then wavers;
makes an effort, unable to look away, to lift
her arms towards his neck; they falter
and fall at her side.    The two stand spell-
bound by mutual recognition.    Then she
speaks in a low voice.)*

MARY.    Oh, let me go!

*(She turns her head with an effort, — gathers
her cloak about her, then hastens out as if
from some terror.)*

*(The Player is alone beside the chimney-piece.
The street outside is darkening with twilight
through the casements and upper door.    There
is a sound of rough-throated singing that
comes by and is softened with distance.    It
breaks the spell.)*

THE PLAYER.    So; it is over . . . now. (*He
looks into the fire.*)

.    .    .    .    .    .    .

"*Fair, kind, and true.*"    *And true!* . . . My golden
Friend.
Those two . . . together. . . . He was ill at ease.
But that he should betray me with a kiss!

.    .    .    .    .    .    .

By this preposterous world . . . I am in need.
Shall there be no faith left ?    Nothing but names?
Then he's a fool who steers his life by such.

Why not the body-comfort of this herd
Of creatures huddled here to keep them warm? —
Trying to drown out with enforcèd laughter
The query of the winds . . . unanswered winds
That vex the soul with a perpetual doubt.
What holds me ? . . . Bah, that were a Cause,
        indeed !
To prove your soul one truth, by being it, —
Against the foul dishonor of the world !
How else prove aught ? . . .

                              I talk into the air.
And at my feet, my honor full of wounds.
Honor ?   Whose honor ?   For I knew my sin,
And she . . . had none.   There's nothing to
        avenge.

> (*He speaks with more and more passion, too
> distraught to notice interruptions.   Enter
> Dickon, with a tallow-dip.   He regards The
> Player with half-open mouth from the cor-
> ner ; then stands by the casement, leaning up
> against it and yawning now and then.*)

I had no right : that I could call her mine
So none should steal her from me, and die for't.
There's nothing to avenge . . . Brave beggary !
How fit to lodge me in this home of Shows,
With all the ruffian life, the empty mirth,
The gross imposture of humanity,
Strutting in virtues it knows not to wear,

Knave in a stolen garment — all the same —
Until it grows enamored of a life
It was not born to, — falls a-dream, poor cheat,
In the midst of its native shams, — the thieves and
    bears
And ballad-mongers all ! . . . Of such am I.
    *(Reënter Tobias and one or two taverners.*
      *Tobias regards The Player, who does not*
      *notice any one, — then leads off Dickon by*
      *the ear. Exeunt into tap-room. The Player*
      *goes to the casement, pushes it wide open, and*
      *gazes out at the sky.*
Is there nought else? . . . I could make shift to
    bind
My heart up and put on my mail again,
To cheat myself and death with one fight more,
If I could think there were some worldly use
For bitter wisdom.
                But I'm no general,
That my own hand-to-hand with evil days
Should cheer my doubting thousands . . .
                          I'm no more
Than one man lost among a multitude ;
And in the end dust swallows them — and me,
And the good sweat that won our victories.
Who sees ? Or seeing, cares ? Who follows on ?
Then why should my dishonor trouble me,
Or broken faith in him ? *What is it suffers ?*
*And why ?* Now that the moon is turned to blood.

(*He turns towards the door with involuntary
longing, and seems to listen.*)

No . . . no, he will not come.  Well, I have
    nought
To do but pluck from me my bitter heart,
And live without it.

> (*Reënter Dickon with a tankard and a cup.
> He sets them down on a small table; this he
> pushes towards The Player, who turns at the
> noise.*)

                  So . . .?  Is it for me?

DICKON.   Ay, on the score!  I had good sight
    o' the bear.

Look, here's a sprig was stuck on him with
    pitch; —

> (*Rubbing the sprig on his sleeve*)

I caught it up, — from Lambeth marsh, belike.
Such grow there, and I've seen thee cherish
    such.

THE PLAYER.   Give us thy posy.

> (*He comes back to the fire and sits in the chair
> near by.  Dickon gets out the iron lantern
> from the corner.*)

DICKON.                 Hey!  It wants a light.

> (*The Player seems to listen once more, his face
> turned towards the door.  He lifts his hand
> as if to hush Dickon, lets it fall, and looks
> back at the fire.  Dickon regards him with
> shy curiosity and draws nearer.*)

DICKON.    Thou wilt be always minding of the
    fire . . .
Wilt thou not?
    THE PLAYER.    Ay.
    DICKON.            It likes me, too.
    THE PLAYER.                    So?
    DICKON.                            Ay. . . .
I would I knew what thou art thinking on
When thou dost mind the fire. . . .
    THE PLAYER.            Wouldst thou?
    DICKON.                            Ay.
        (*Sound of footsteps outside. A group ap-
        proaches the door.*)
Oh, here he is, come back!
    THE PLAYER (*rising with passionate eagerness*).
                Brave lad — brave lad!
    DICKON (*singing*).
        *Hang out your lanthorns, trim your lights*
        *To save your days from knavish nights!*
        (*He plunges, with his lantern, through the
        doorway, stumbling against Wat Burrow,
        who enters, a sorry figure, the worse for
        wear.*)
    WAT (*sourly*).    Be the times soft, that you
    must try to cleave
Way through my ribs as tho' I was the moon? —
And you the man-wi'-the-lanthorn, or his dog? —
You bean! . . (*Exit Dickon. Wat shambles in
    and sees The Player.*)

What, you sir, here ?

THE PLAYER.   Ay, here, good Wat.   (*While Wat crosses to the table and gets himself a chair, The Player looks at him as if with a new consciousness of the surroundings.   After a time he sits as before.   Reënter Dickon and curls up on the floor, at his feet.*)

WAT.   O give me comfort, sir.   This cursèd day, —

A wry, damned . . . noisome. . . . Ay, poor Nick, poor Nick !

He's all to mend — Poor Nick !   He's sorely maimed,

More than we'd baited him with forty dogs.

'Od's body !   Said I not, sir, he would fight ?

Never before had he, in leading-chain,

Walked out to take the air and show his parts. . . .

'Went to his noddle like some greenest gull's

That's new come up to town. . . . The prentices

Squeaking along like Bedlam, he breaks loose

And prances me a hey, — I dancing counter !

Then such a cawing 'mongst the women !   Next,

The chain did clatter and enrage him more ; —

You would 'a' sworn a bear grew on each link,

And after each a prentice with a cudgel, —

Leaving him scarce an eye !   So, howling all,

We run a pretty pace . . . and Nick, poor Nick,

He catches on a useless, stumbling fry

That needed not be born, — and bites into him.

And then . . . the Constable . . . And now, no
    show !
   THE PLAYER.    Poor Wat ! . . . Thou went-
    est scattering misadventure
Like comfits from thy horn of plenty, Wat.
   WAT.    Ay, thank your worship.    You be
    best to comfort.    (*He pours a mug of ale.*)
No show to-morrow !    Minnow Constable. . . .
I'm a jack-rabbit strung up by my heels
For every knave to pinch as he goes by !
Alas, poor Nick, bear Nick . . . oh, think on
    Nick.
   THE PLAYER.    With all his fortunes darkened
    for a day, —
And the eye o' his reason, sweet intelligencer,
Under a beggarly patch. . . . I pledge thee, Nick.
   WAT.    Oh, you have seen hard times, sir, with
    us all.
Your eyes lack lustre, too, this day.    What say you ?
No jesting. . . . What ?    I've heard of marvels
    there
In the New Country.    There would be a knop-
    hole
For thee and me.    There be few Constables
And such unhallowed fry. . . . An thou wouldst
    lay
Thy wit to mine — what is't we could not do ?
Wilt turn't about ?    (*Leans towards him in cordial
    confidence.*)

                      Nay, you there, sirrah boy,
Leave us together; as 'tis said in the play,
' Come, leave us, Boy ! '

      (*Dickon does not move. He gives a sigh and
          leans his head against The Player's knee, his
          arms around his legs. He sleeps. The
          Player gazes sternly into the fire, while Wat
          rambles on, growing drowsy.*)

WAT. The cub there snores good counsel.
    When all's done,
What a bubble is ambition ! . . . When all's
    done . .
What's yet to do ? . . . Why, sleep. . . . Yet
    even now
I was on fire to see myself and you
Off for the Colony with Raleigh's men.
I've been beholden to 'ee. . . . Why, for thee
I could make shift to suffer plays o' Thursday.
Thou'rt the best man among them, o' my word.
There's other trades and crafts and qualities
Could serve . . . an thou wouldst lay thy wit to
    mine.
Us two ! . . . us two ! . . .

    THE PLAYER (*apart, to the fire*). " Fair, kind,
    and true." . . .

    WAT.              . . . Poor Nick !

      (*He nods over his ale. There is muffled noise
          in the tap-room. Some one opens the door a
          second, letting in a stave of a song, then slams*

*the door shut.   The Player, who has turned,*
*gloomily, starts to rise.   Dickon moves in his*
*sleep, sighs heavily, and settles his cheek*
*against The Player's shoes.   The Player looks*
*down for a moment.   Then he sits again,*
*looking now at the fire, now at the boy, whose*
*hair he touches.)*

THE PLAYER.   So, heavy-head.   You bid me
   think  my thought
Twice over; keep me by, a heavy heart,
As ballast for thy dream.  Well, I will watch . . .
Like slandered Providence.   Nay, I'll not be
The prop to fail thy trust untenderly,
After a troubled day. . . .

                 Nay, rest you here.


        CURTAIN.

# POEMS

# THE SOURCE

I KNOW, whatever God may be,
  All Life it was that lighted me
This little flame whereby I see.

I know All Strength did stir this hand
To serve somehow the poor command
Of whatsoe'er I understand.

And from All Love there throbs the stress
Of pity and of wistfulness
Both to be blessèd and to bless.

Then by the Source that still doth pour
On star and glow-worm reckoned for,
I will have more and ever more!

## THE QUIET

NOW the roads, hushed with dark,
   Lead the homeward way,
I will rest ; I will hark
   What the weeds can say ;
Wondering in the afterglow,
   Heart's-ease of the day.

One day more, one day more.
   Ay, if it were new !
There the city smoke goes soft,
   Melting in the blue ;
And the highways, vext with dust,
   Heal them in the dew.

Am I wise — am I dull
   To put off despair,
But because the mist floats up
   From the pastures there,
Like the fellow breath of toil,
   Warm upon the air ?

One day more, — one day more ;
   Ay, and what to come ?
Nothing answers, though I doubt ;
   All the trees are dumb :

But the primrose stands alight,
    And the flocks are home.

Underneath the little moon,
    Sharp and sweet to see,
All the warm, listless herbs
    Send a breath to me;
And the fields bide, in peace,
    Harvest-time to be.

Still the shadows close and come,
    Like a friendly herd,
And the summer twilight broods
    Tranquil as a bird;
And the brook tells her quest,
    By the silver word.

Still the murmurs overflow,
    Fold me with a spell;
And the distance sends a call
    Dimly, in the bell . . .
When to pipe,— when to weep,
    Do I know so well?

I have seen drought and dearth,
    Yet the Spring's secure;
And the work was long, and lone;
    But the past is sure.
And the hill-tops see beyond,
    And the stars endure.

Often when the thing I wrought
   Wore not as I would,
When my need had left me bare
   To the season's mood,
Yet the heavy heart in me
   Saw that it was good.

I have seen Joy take leave
   With a bitter guise:
Griefs have had a smile for me,
   When I met their eyes.
Who shall know with what new gift
   Life may make me wise?

Be it savors of the dusk
   Sooth my care in me,
Or the trees, that bid me wait
   What the hills foresee,
There the fields bide in peace
   Harvest yet to be.

Oh, the wiser way of them!
   Doubt has nought to say.
Shall I reason deeper, I,
   Moulded from the clay?
Rather will I trust the dark,
   Heart's-ease of the day.

## THE PSYCHE IN THE NICHE

I KNOW not by what way I came
  To poise the silver singing flame
Uplifted here; and though I guess,
It is a lonely blessedness.
But bowered white with spheral calms,
I see the wild-flowers and the palms
  They offer — passing by the shrine —
  Before whose need even I may shine,
  An almoner of peace not mine.

I know not why it gives them ease
To bring me all their memories;
Or why I seem, to men forspent,
A mystical enlightenment.
But since 'tis so, be sure I take
Their sorrow, gladly, for love's sake.
  I bind their burdens in a sheaf;
  I hold my arms out unto grief
  And hallow it, with flower and leaf.

I keep the broken things that were
Too many, for a wanderer :
The hope outworn, the heavier stress,
The savors of rare bitterness

From dreams too fine for daily bread;
And in my heart their wounds are red.
   The spirit's mute indwelling tear
   Is mine; nor could I hold as dear
   The first rapt snowdrop of the year!


They pass and pass.   And sweet it is
To guard unheeded mysteries,
Like roots that Spring shall bring to be
A thousand-petaled fragancy!
And sweet it is to be the cool,
Forgotten haunt, all beautiful
   For once, unto the eyes of pain
   That, healèd once with living rain,
   Pass by and never come again.


Sometimes the taper shrinks and flares
Beneath a whirlwind of despairs
That poise and circle, night and day;
And scarce my anguished fingers may
Withhold a little, lovely spark
From that fierce hunger of the Dark, —
   The outcry of some groaning deep
   Calling upon me without sleep,
   That I let fall the light, and weep!


And weep I would . . . save that I must
The more, the more, lift eyes of trust

(As sometimes you may smile into
The folding sky, unanswering blue)
For very need of loyalty,
To something that I never see
But love, although it give no sign :
Some radiance hid, some Heart, divine,
That is far lonelier than mine.

## I SHALL ARISE

YOU doubt.   And yet, O you who walk your
      ways
Glad of your very breath !
Look back along the days :
Have you not tasted death ?

What of the hour of anguish, over-past,
So fierce, so lone,
That even now the Soul looks back aghast
At sorrow of its own :
The piercèd hands and stark, —
The eyes gone dark ?
You who have known
And trodden down the fangs of such defeat,
Did you not feel some veil of flesh sore rent, —
Then, wonderment ?
Did you not find it sweet
To live, still live, — to see, to breathe again,
Victorious over pain ?
Did you not feel once more, as darkness went,
Upon your forehead, cold with mortal dew,
The daybreak new ?
And far and new, some eastern breath of air
From that rapt Garden where

The lilies stood new-risen, fragranter
Than myrrh?

" Death, Death, was this thy sting —
This bitter thing?
Can it be past?
Only I know there was one agony,
One strait way to pass by,
A stress that could not last.
And in such conflict, something had to die . . .
It was not I."

## THE KNOT

I DID not love you, and I ever said
  I did not love you.  So the end was told.
How did it happen with so strait a theme
The days could play their winding harmonies,
With ritornello?  Oh, I hated me,
That when I loved you not, yet I could feel
Some charm in me the deeper for your love;
Some singing-robe invisible — and spun
Of your own worship — fold me silverly
In very moonlight, so that I walked fair
When you were by, who had no wish to be
The fairer for your eyes!  But at some cost
Of other life the hyacinth grows blue,
And sweetens ever. . . . So it is with us,
The sadder race.  I would have fled from you;
And yet I felt some fibre in myself
Binding me here, to search one moment yet —
The only well that gave me back a star, —
Your eyes reflecting.  And I grew aware
How worship that must ever spend and burn,
Will have its deity, from gold or stone;
Till that fain womanhood that would be fair
And lovable, — the hunger of the plant,
Against my soul's commandment reached and took
The proffered fruit, more potent day by day.

Oh, it was not an artful lowered brow!
The lifted eyelash would have seemed to you
Desirable, or shadowed backward look.
I warn you in a dream.   My own heart hears,
Cold and far-off, unhastened, curious,
A sea-plant fed with alien element, —
Watching through twilight eyes some underwave.
Will you not go ? . . .
                        And yet, why will you go ?

## GHOST

IF you are loath to have me standing here
Gray on your dark, a blur against the noon,
Why did you make me This? . . . I cannot choose
But face you so with unaccusing eyes
Of knowledge, now I see you as you are, —
To wonder how I saw you as I did,
Too long unknowing. I am filled with wonder,
Poising between the Outer Place and you,
Held changeless with the laughter dimly here,
So sudden blasted. Yes, and I would go,
If it might be; but this one gift it seems
I may not bribe of death or destiny.
I cannot buy you peace with aught I have,
Even forgiveness . . . now that all is done.
That was the last way to be rid of me.
Not willingly I gaze on you and Hate,
With this same "Wherefore, wherefore?" It is
    true
The murdered heart will ever bleed again,
When one draws near: no other touch, but one,
Can start the bitter drops from dead amaze!

You who would have me gone — both then and
    now —
I would be gone from you. And I would lose

This gleam of stricken laughter from my eyes ;
Because death made me older, and I see
How little cause there was in me for mirth.
Only I never guessed ; I was so dull —
Looking for love — and knew not of this thing.
I see all now. . . . *Ah, Silent One, how long*
*Must we look on each other, face to face ?*

## IN THE SILENCE

WHERE didst Thou tarry, Lord, Lord,
     Who heeded not my prayer?
All the long day, all the long night,
     I stretched my hands to air.

"There was a bitterer want than thine
     Came from the frozen North;
Laid hands upon My garment's hem
     And led Me forth.

"It was a lonely Northern man:
     Where there was never tree
To shed its comfort on his heart,
     There he had need of Me.

"He kindled us a little flame
     To hope against the storm;
And unto him, and unto Me,
     The light was warm."

And yet I called Thee, Lord, Lord—
     Who answered not, nor came:
All the long day, and yesterday,
     I called Thee by Thy name.

" There was a dumb, unhearing grief
    Spake louder than thy word.
There was a heart called not on Me;
    But yet I heard.

" The sorrow of a savage man
    Shaping him gods, alone,
Who found no love in the shapen clay
    To answer to his own.

" His heart knew what his eyes saw not;
    He bade Me stay, and eat;
And unto him, and unto Me,
    The cup was sweet.

" Too long we wait for thee and thine,
    In sodden ways and dim.
And where the man's need cries on Me,
    There have I need of him.

" Along the borders of despair
    Where sparrows seek no nest,
Nor ravens food, I sit at meat,
    — The unnamed Guest."

## THE SURVIVOR

I WILL not drown my day in grief,
  But I shall breast the tide, and know;
And knowledge shall not make me brief,
But I will eat thereof and grow.

One happiness shall not possess
The freeborn soul I was before;
But I will drink down happiness
With a good heart, and call for more!

My brain may crave for knowledge, chief,
Though I am more than brain indeed;
My present need will have its grief,
Though I am more than present need.

And heart, with hunger never less,
May scorn all ministries apart,
Imploring for its happiness:
But I am greater than my heart.

## THE VIOLIN WITHHELD

### I

THE Song, at last unfolded, curve on curve,
  Blooms to completion, and as lilies close,
Folds it in silence.   So, with all the light,
It goes . . .
No echo more; the memory must serve,
O vain to hark!——
The sweet, unpitying reticence of night:
Silence again, and dark.

To hear a music waning from my need,
It is to me
Bereavement.   So the native shores recede
With all the faces dearest to a heart,
When it is time to part,
Not to be stayed,—— fading relentlessly.
I watch the waters widen, I who know
How far I go.

### II

All gone, all dark, the welcome and the dream
Of a lost godhead that was mine indeed;
Some source of all remembrances supreme,
And common with the planets and the seed.

Nigh to the heart of Light, I heard it send
Light throbbing without end
Through mist on mist, —
Colors and calls and echoed potencies
For earth and moon and seas.
Hooded with tempest, hovered at my wrist
The falcon lightning. . . . Oh, I heard and saw
Familiar glories, greeted with no awe,
But human tears:
The ebb and flow of tide on tide of years;
The days like petals budding and unfurled;
The building of the World.
And then the making, — from what troubled clay,
Veined with the reddest dawn of summer day,
Sun-kindled with the flame to be, to seek, —
The Wonderful and Weak!

Then, for the little hour, a vagrant god
Brooding upon resplendent memories
The while he rests beside his path untrod,
With shadowed eyes,
I too — I too looked forth upon the Earth,
A child of royal birth,
And felt the proud assurance of my own,
In face of all wild beauty;— none so wild
Or beautiful, but had for me, the child,
Some look of home; for me —
With stranger ways, and threadbare and alone,
And shod so painfully.

" I knew you, Glories, in some outer place.
Oh, scorn not me, you rapturous wayside face
Of rose, that hast the lore from that brown earth,
What it is worth
To thrill you so and flush you fairer far
Than human faces are,
Flushing so transiently.
Rich breath, the life I was and I shall be —
Some day when I am come into my own —
Looks on you now, through eyes that compre-
     hend
Beginning wrought with end,
Or ever you were, and when you shall be gone;
(And whither, what wind knows ?)
Yea, dear, my Rose."

Clear sung.   But while I muse, with eager eyes
     on
The vision that fulfills,
The one wild-bee that showed me pathway home
Is gone with daylight: down the mists are come
To cheat me out of knowledge of the hills,
And hide horizon.

### III

My Violin, if I could call thee mine,
Interpreter,
I dream all ways were plain, all lovelier,

Through that soothsay of thine;
And how I should be led
By the sure quest of such a golden thread,
Through all vext mazes ; beckonèd along
Through Dark, a glory, — Silence, mother song,
Where harbors every omen that eludes,
The hidden tryst of all beatitudes, ·
All joys that none may capture or foresee.
And it will never be.

Oh, but some clew there must be here to wind
Through these appalling darknesses, that bind
The baffled heart in with dismay and doubt ;
To lead us out
Unto a source, a first all-meaning Word,
Sure to enfold like some dear blinding hand
Of love shut in upon the rebel bird
That cannot understand!
Some farther voice must say
The path is there, though it be far withdrawn ;
As if a child should point us out the way
To Eden, in the dawn.

And for the lives that own nor clew nor seer
To tell the meaning clear,
Whom Beauty startles as a newcomer
Shy in the door, — and they as shy to her —
For whom her foreign speech
Wakens a wistful pain too strange to teach,

For them the groping thought,
Unvalued and unsought,
Lives dark : until the chance interpreter,
The Song unfolding to a soundless call,
Most wonderful, says all ;
At last, says all — . . . and then,
As lilies fold again,
Even with the day that shone, —
Is gone.

## IV

Yet, is it wasted, that which wells unseen, —
Escape that might have been ?
The voice withheld, can vision wither so ?
Shall not the risen longing overflow
Unto the needs
Of joyless duties, thronging parched and low
Along the days, like weeds ?
May it not be, for them that find no speech,
The life unlived, the love unloved, the stress
Of thwarted songfulness,
The very reach
Of heart's desire, the utmost urge of want,
Shall find a way to grace
Poor hours, grown dull and gaunt
With longing for new day,
For sight of some far place ? —
Dreamers of destined joy gone all astray.

(Heart's dim possession that the hands resign, —
My Violin, not mine !)

Ah, that which finds release when others sing,
Dies never so.
My World, thy great heart cannot hold the Spring
Long hid.   The grass will know.

## LITANY OF THE LIVING

*Death, thou hast taken.*
*Death, thou dost give.*
*We who outlive,*
*Lo, we awaken!*

### I

NOW that it is too late,
We watch, who never saw.
We listen with vain awe;
We long: we wait.
Time looks so desolate,
Time that we hoarded once.
And something blunts
The sense of leisure now, where none intrudes,
The ample solitudes
Of vacant days.
Come, let us consecrate
To his new state
Rich hours and hours with memory and praise,
Now that it is too late.

### II

Surely we are grown wise
With these amazèd eyes,

Yes, we are eager, glad,
To sum up all we had,
Remember, count and glory!   We divine
Full well our riches in the day of cost.
All that we had, thou makest it to shine,
Since it is lost.
This, then, was he.
At last we heed, — we see,
Resistless!
We see all things so clear;
And where we heard not, hear,
And love where we were listless.

> *Death, potent Healer,*
> *Death, who dost give,*
> *Hear us that live,*
> *Unblessed Revealer!*

## III

By the dear price we paid
For hearts new made,
Oh, by this searing light,
This anguish of new sight,
Let not our wisdom fade.
Grant us to understand
These near at hand: —
Oh, while the sand still runs,
To cherish and to feed

Their living need.
We frugal ones !
We who put off from maddened day to day
The word to say : —
We who are ever dumb
Rather than waste the crumb !

Sting to some human use of new discerning,
Our shamèd learning ;
To greet all beauties, perfect or begun,
While there is sun ;
To gladden and to thank all shadowed graces
In hidden wistful places ;
To give, to give ; to trust,
Before their hearts are dust,
And ours undone.

Thou showest where we err.
But O, Interpreter ! —
Pointing the meaning of this piteous Book
Whereon we look,
Let us be wise some day to understand ;
To understand indeed,
And see, and read, —
Without thy Hand.

## EPISTLES

### I

*Memorable*

MY Very Dear, the crescent moon
Will whiten soon,
A drifting petal, bitter-sweet to see;
And in the western sky
The golden islands lie,
Too far for me.

The tree-tops are astir:
Aspen and birch, and fir,
And pine the murmurer.

Beyond and still beyond, in that dim croon
Of fields that wait the moon,
Where the moths hover,
There stand a-muse for any primrose-lover
The lights that bide, —
A solace for the going of the sun:
Meek fragrancies
Tacit and golden-eyed!

All, all and more than these,
The lovely Dark gives to the seeker's eye,

But one by one.
And I must tell you though I know not why,
Save that you always hear, —
My Very Dear.

## II
### *To A. F. B. in Praise of Us.*

What are We Two ? — that whatsoever way
We meet, at morning, noon, or eventide,
Though yesterday had seen us side by side,
A new year has come in since yesterday !
" *What's new, o'heaven's name, to do or say ?* "
The elders wonder at us, open-eyed.
Care slips, and grief — the pack — is swung aside ;
And work must needs be done, but not to-day.

*Aha !* However 'tis, some sudden bloom
Of Arden bowers over us, serene,
While to the thousand murmurs of her loom
Kind Summer sings, a-making leaves of green.
And how we laugh, we lucky ones, for whom
Bubble all laughters hitherto unseen !

## III
### *To the Friend that Was.*

Yes, you : the only one to say " Not I ! "
To the abiding query of a glance ;

Yes, you who ever choose to look askance
At proffered hands of welcome, and pass by.
You know you cannot be my enemy
Longer than some poor cloud-time of mischance
Blots, by your will, the ageless countenance
Of a blue heaven that bids you answer Why.

But ah, the waste of time!   And, once Outside,
How shall we see the futile raindrop, hurled
Into the bosom of that radiant daytime?
Yet must I grieve at any grace denied, —
For all the lost bright weathers in the world,
And the vain shadow on this mortal Maytime.

## THE HEARER

I listen; and I listen; and surmise.
 I listen to all musics that may be;
And to the shapes and faces that my eyes
                See.

I listen for the strains of daily fate
To merge into some large assurèd Song;
Yea! though belief, and hope, and hunger wait
                . . . Long.

And more than all, I listen to the deep
Of Silences that fold it all around,
Petal on petal, to the heart asleep,
                Sound.

Yet am I dumb: until She blow the breath —
Here on my forehead — of a spheral spring;
And Her eyes veil; and the near silence saith,
                "Sing."

## THE WINGLESS JOY

YES, it is beautiful. . . . There is no man
　　Living who could have made the thing so
　　　plain
For eyes untaught : and there his work is great.
He loved life best in marble.　But 'twas Life,
Breath, impulse, passion — name it as you will —
He chose apart from Dream.　No paradox :
It's not the maker, primitive himself,
Who knows the beauty of his simpleness.
The subtle man, the thwarted modern man
It is who sees the old instinctive life
With eyes of curious envy ; holds aloof
To study with delight the primal hues
And pulsing shadow and clear symmetries
Of stress and joy and folly, not for him —
Thought-hindered and complex.　That man was
　　Niel.


But how he made her !　I have loitered here
Along the gallery, of a holiday,
And watched the workmen passing, twos and threes,
To see the sights, half-looking with grave awe
On this and that (freemen and yet oppressed
By some vague condescension of the air)

Turn back, to finger a companion's sleeve
And point at this.  It needs no word at all
To tell the meaning of the Wingless Joy.

Unto the happiest life, the gods allow
But once that rapture tiptoe in mid-heaven!
And yet she is so sweetly made of earth,
The earth of rain-pure April — and her lips
Are parted with a human sweet amaze
To feel the sudden immortality
Of flame go singing, singing in her veins,
" Kin with the rose-tree and the wakened brook,
Made to make glad, behold I gladden You,
And all things lean to me !  I cannot die."
How simple, just to make her standing there,
Poised like a fountain, ever old and new !
And her wide eyes — some statues have no eyes —
Rapt with the tidings of exceeding joy
That dawns for her, a vision half withheld
Of utmost, and unspeakable, and dear ;
Herself so clear a heart, she cannot doubt !
For me, that woman wrought of changeless stone,
Darkles and sparkles with a living light.
Her smile so questions something her eyes see
And read again.  Her revelation grows ;
And how the risen gladness overruns
From her glad being, — sweetness of the tree,
To thrill the air and hold it like a Voice !

Some look askance upon that gift of his
To seize ephemera and make them live ; —
Call it unsculpturesque . . . although his art
Hushes the cricket-cry like thunder near,
When they stand face to face with such as this,
This Utmost Moment that outlives the years.

.        .        .        .        .        .        .

Wingless, you see.   She has no other home.
She loves her once; the single soul of her
Knows but the glory of one day and night.
She may not come and go, — nor hide, nor range;
Nor find her any refuge in the stars.
She walks the earth with lovely earthly feet,
And when earth fails her, she can only die.
How well he knew ! . . .   And yet he did not
        know.

You've heard the story.   But you never saw
The woman till to-day ; well, see her now.
And yet if you had seen her that first time
She dawned on us. . . . A knock upon the door,
Half-heeded with " Come in " — and there she
        stood,
Full in a shaft of sunlight that the square
Small window of the hall let in, with Spring.
Her eyes unknowing, wide and unafraid,
And the whole outline of her edged with light;
Her hair, — you know that dark of Italy,
So black, it turns the sun to silverness,

And in the shadow, purples with a bloom
Of vineyards ?   And you know the brightness held
In the warm shallow of a woman's ear,
So intricate and simple, — human rose,
But eloquent as not a rose may be !
Oh, yes, for that first breath, you may be sure
I thought the Vision must have given heed,
Quite mother-wise, like the Madonna there
Who holds her Baby ever in her arm
And listens to the prayers of all the poor !
This seemed so plain a challenge from the Sun,
Color and color !   Such a little thing
Remained — to paint it merely — in the day
Of visitation !   I was wrong, you see.
Enough of dreamers. . . . It was Life for Niel ;
And it was Niel who saw her Beauty through
The clothing loveliness ; and it was Niel
Who made her clear : — the elemental heart
That can drink off one rapture for a draught,
Mindless of meat and drink forevermore.

       .       .       .       .       .       .       .

That first day keeps the fragrance more than all.
I know Niel watched her with his opaque eyes
Of thought, while she, her errand on her lips,
Unuttered, moved about half dreamingly,
A shy, sure presence ; looked upon his work
And then at mine, with the first smile for me ;
Stood back an instant from Diskobolos,
In a dark corner, then begged pardon of him

Speechlessly with a slow approving look
Of old acquaintance; passed the Laughing Faun;
Wondered somewhat, with gentle courtesy,
At the scant treasures that our walls could show
In those bare days (for we were workmen both);
The few old textiles, prey of moth and dust,
But boastful of their color to the last;
A sketch or two from dead, immortal hands,
And hanging near, a crescent in a wrack
Of sunset-cloud, my eastern scimitar.
Whereat she shook her head and drew her breath —
As a good child helps out a fairy tale
With willing fright — and drew away from it.
Then catching sight of some more friendly thing,
Her eyes grew gold again with happy mirth;
She flung the shawl back from her little wrist,
Spread wide the fingers, tapered like a saint's,
And held them, warm and fresh, beside a cast
As like as death may be . . . " So, here, — my
        hand!"
Out came the errand then by single words,
Strange music to us, scattered mellow notes,
And then a rush of voluble sweet talk,
Like the first blackbird that a schoolboy hears.

I think he saw his triumph from the first,
This venture that would win the world to him,
While he made studies, and the problem grew.
The workman in him breasted, day and night,

A stretch of bush and brier and stubborn rock
Fit for a pioneer; — won inch by inch,
As none could do who did not see his path
Through one portentous struggle, to the clear
Far peak, star-confident.   Niel was a man
Who bound the service of all elements
He came upon : himself unpitied slave
To his own purpose, — other minds to him ;
This girl beyond them all. . . .
No, there is nothing hidden, no offence
Unsightly to the world ; — all far from that !
Of course she came to love him, to be his
As wholly as a dumb child must belong
To its interpreter.   He had the look
That comprehends a man, and binds him so.
For Niel there was no mystery in men :
No need to be yourself adventurer !
Art for Art's sake ! and keep your vision clear :
Lean from the gallery along with us
And watch the gladiators as they come,
And praise who dies the best !   We are beyond
That rude encounter, beautiful to see.
He understood it so, and took delight
In nature of the simplest human scale.
The unknown essence only served to spice
Some little talk of self, across the smoke,
Late evenings ; filled the place of reverence
Towards women of his world, elusive, fine,
Detached as he, between their ways of thought

And outgrown intuitions.    Ah, he was
An Artist; and he saw as none else could,
The rarity of this intrepid bloom
Whose only speech was Being.    There it grew
Wild, by the highroad !    And he gathered it.

I do not know how much of it was Art,
Or how much more, perhaps, the constant lure
Of her young spirit for the curious mind.
It is not often that we see a heart
So near — and red — and empty.    And to know —
To know for once, and show it to the world,
How golden eyes could darken and turn gold
From some new source of sunrise and of night;
To see a child-face grow before your own
Into the dream of womanhood in flower ;
To know what words that simple tongue would shape
For tenderness as foreign as its speech ; —
To know what Eve could find in her to say
When first the lips of the first man made plea
Against her cheek, there in the garden-place,
Eastward in Eden — have you ever thought ? —
Herself the only woman that she knew !
Did you not wish, along the gallery there
Only an hour ago, to take that vase
Of Cyprus out from all its fellow wares,
Into the light, where you could hear it plain ? —
You said so, laughing, — where it could unfold
Its eloquence ; the equal melody,

And the globed dimness, glass soft breathed upon
By ancient years till it is opal-strange,
And lucent as a drowsy underwave
Of green sea-water lighted by the sun;
Perfect and empty : — with some use, be sure,
Save to stand idle, even for us to see
With eyes of worship.    For the elder Art
Had ever such near kinship with men's lives,
To enrich poor shrines and sweeten peasant bread.
So, why not make that shape articulate?
Fulfil its longing; set it in the light;
Give it the crocuses it's empty for,
And watch the water, softly set ajar,
Shake out the beryl lights and filminess,
And gather silver on the April stems.
The love of some men is not so unlike
This woman fineness.    Yes, all thought aside,
To watch the beauty of fulfilment, close,
With pleased and curious eyes.
                                        I saw — half saw —
How Niel was making her the perfect Joy
With all a workman's ardor of research.
God knows I cannot tell what art he used . . .
My voice is not the charmer's —    But I saw
He would have out the hidden strength in her, —
Bade her be woman; — studied with delight
The early largess of that southern dawn;
Blew back the folded petals of the rose,
Only to see! . . . till he could say at last,

" Look at me, Benedetta.   So, at me.
And can you look, for just the breathing space,
As if you saw before you — but not far,
All that your heart desired ; — not too far —
The dearest thing that you could ask of life ?
Yes, see it, try to see the Heart's Desire ! "
His hands upon her shoulders then, for poise ;
And as she looked back dumbly (coming in,
I seemed to hear her look) he tried too far
What tenderness could wake.   "So, child," he
        said,
And kissed her.

The model grew like magic from that day ; —
The world knows how, and how it saw the light.
At the first cry of that world-wide acclaim,
She shared our little carnival with us ;
And kissed her radiant sister of the clay —
Because she brought him fortune in an hour ! —
And kissed her own face in the faded glass,
Saying, " Yes, it is true, the thing you speak :
The good God made my head and hands and all ;
He made me well.   But you," — to Niel, — " you,
        you,
Have made me much more lovelier than He.
Oh, Benedetta !   She is Joy indeed ! "

.    .    .    .    .    .

Within a few strange weeks, how all was changed
After his years of shallow half-success,

The venture won, the man's name common talk,
And the One Woman of his finer world —
Charmed from herself and stepping from the niche
To follow his new fortunes over sea !
It seems a thing unreal, impossible
To dreamer and to drudge.   But so it came.
On the last day I found him there at work
Against the sudden break for liberty,
Ready to go.   I spoke then: "Does she know?"
"Who?   Benedetta?   Yes, she must have heard,
These noisy days that I have been away.
She is a marvel, when all's said.   Without her
It never could have been.   I owe her all. —
A genius for existence. . . . What she might
Have been . . . in any other century !
Well, she's herself : a glory.   And for me,
The thing is done."
                          I was still there at dusk,
Unwillingly delaying, when she came.
"The marble, Benedetta!   It is sold."
She listened dully, creature of the South,
Sleep-walking in some desolate new cold;
Her eyes too fixed with watching.   So : she knew.
"Me — me," she answered slowly, "that is well.
You have your fortune of it.   I am glad.
And you are going — where?"
                          "New lands. — new seas ;
Your country, Benedetta!"
                          "Yes," she said,

" It was my country : I remember it. . . .
And when you go, you take the clay with you ? "
He laughed a little.   " Say good-by," he said,
" Like the good friend you are, and wish me well.
I cannot tell you what you were to me. . . .
I go to-morrow. . . . "   I have never seen
Before or since that day such eyes of death,
Wide, empty, gaunt — with all the light gone out.
He answered half, the gaze he did not meet
Even with his own  opaque and buoyant looks —
Turned to the Joy and said, " Look, you are she !
Be proud of her, for she is always glad."

For a strange moment, then, she stretched her arms
Like one left houseless, saying, " *Is it I ?* "
And looked at her two hands, and at the Joy
That smiled on her unwisdom, with great eyes.
And feeling, with vague steps, and sight gone dim,
After the doorway, — so she chanced to jar
The single hanging with its bits of steel ;
And sound and thought struck home.

                              I know it was
A madness, not a purpose ; nay, not that, —
Only the impulse of a tortured heart
To put some thing that suffered out of pain :
She caught that lightning from the tapestry.

   .     .     .     .     .     .     .

My scimitar it was. . . . I drew it out.
But time seemed long with nothing left to do

Save bite the anguish back, to succor hers,
And kiss her poor sweet hands, and lay her down,
— The torn heart in her harshly sobbing out
Its redness, — and to turn her face away
From that transfigured vision of herself,
Still smiling on her . . . as it smiles on you.
And this is what she lived for ! . . .

                                    I was wrong
To call him Judas.   How should he foresee ?
The spirit is grown frugal in these days.
Who thinks to meet with spendthrift love and hate
Out of a sonnet sequence ? — What, at home ?
Or in the street ?   Or in your eyes, new friend ?
Suppose you set yourself, half poet-wise,
Half curiously, and beckoned by *What-if ?*
To call up some far spirit from Without.
Would not your heart turn cold to see it grow
Reluctantly, — the never-faded eyes,
The voice you disbelieved in, with, " I come.
You called ?   What would you have ? "

                                And yet take care.
We are so quick to blame some Master Hand :
We say, " He made us and He moulded us
To see us broken so ! "   It is the cry
Of the stung believer; and it is the cry
Of him who says there is no God at all, —
Girding up in his heart the bitterness
Against a blank, black space that should be God,
And is not, only emptiness abhorred

By Nature and her son! — We cry on Him.
Oh, why not — if the Art be all in all —
Say of the Potter, "Art for Art's sake," then!
Grant Him your modern right to make and mar
For the mere craft's sake, too; and let Him say,
(Why not, why not?)

      *"I made this Woman here*
*Of fairness from the clay of trodden Springs.*
*Look you, lost June is in her.   You can see*
*In her young hands the selfsame primal glow*
*That flushes in My gardens of the world.*
*And I have given her the miracle,*
*The beating heart within, the holy Fire.*
*So, full of breath. . . . Live, suffer, — shine, and die.*
*Fairer than petals, go the way of them. . . .*
*I made and I have broken.   It is good."*

# SONGS

# DAILY BREAD

WHEN the long gray day is done,
    Spent at weary seams,
Homeward comes my Heart to me,
    With the flock of dreams.

" And what tidings, ruddy Heart ?
    Shall we never share,
Hand in hand, the sun and wind,
    Seeking all that's fair ? "

" Not to-morrow, Dear-to-me !
    Ours are parted ways :
Thine the spinning, mine to seek
    Fortune of the days."

Oh, and it is cold without
    My own Heart to sing ;
Oh, and 'tis a lonely way
    My Heart goes wandering.

But I fold the web, at dusk,
    As a maid beseems ;
And my sunburned Heart comes home,
    With the flock of dreams.

## PLAY UP, PIPER!

PLAY up, play up, my Piper,
   And play the timely song,
The song that never a worker hears,
   Although his heart may long.
It's we are glad to listen here
   Who have but Yea and Nay;
But would you only pipe to us
   The word we want to-day!

We heard your heart-break, Piper;
   And oh, but it was like!
'Tis so — 'tis so, the ill winds blow,
   'Tis so the sorrows strike.
But would you only pipe to us
   The turning of the way,
And how it is you come, at last,
   To pipe again, to-day!

The broken hopes of harvest,
   The wearing of the rain,
The ailing of a little cheek,
   You make us weep again.
But tell us of the wage, man,
   You had for this hard day;
Play up, play up, dear Piper,
   And tell us why you play!

## THE COMFORT

AS I came down along the height
   I saw the Evening Star,
Benignant, near, the nearest lamp
   Among the worlds afar.
Oh, kindly close it looked on me
To keep us children company
   With all love-looks that are!

As I came down along the moor
   I saw the window-light,
Clear shining out across the dark,
   A welcome to the night:
And these two glories, home and star,
The very near and very far,
   Were like to one delight.

As I came by the valley brook
   The fireflies hovered there.
They shed a slow, unanxious glow,
   Poising in quiet air;
So constant and so near at hand
That any eyes could understand
   Their starlight unaware.

Some kinship here I cannot read
   Because it lies too deep:
But these three starry things I saw,
   And mine they are to keep.
How like they were, some happy way, —
It shines through all the troubled day,
   It shines on me through sleep!

## CARPACCIO'S ANGEL WITH
## THE LUTE

I LEAN my head to hear each string:
  We hum together, cheek to cheek,
And oh, there is not anything
  So loud, but I can hear it speak.
And it is shapen like some fruit
All mellowness — my Lute.
       (Wilt sing?)

My singing-bird that I love dear!
  Above the sound of harp and flute
And viol-grown, the voice is clear
  Brown honey from my little Lute.
I harken so to every tone,
Because it is my own.
       (Canst hear?)

## THE STAY-AT-HOME

I HAVE waited, I have longed —
  I have longed as none can know,
All my spring and summer time,
  For this day to come and go;
And the foolish heart was mine,
Dreaming I would see them shine, —
*Harlequin and Columbine*
                    *And Pierrot !*

Now the laughing has gone by,
  On the highway from the inn ;
And the dust has settled down,
  And the house is dead within.
And I stay — who never go —
Looking out upon the snow,
*Columbine and Pierrot*
                    *And Harlequin !*

All the rainbow things you see
  Understream are not so fine;
And their voices weave and cling
  Like my honeysuckle vine,
Lovely as a Violin ! —
Mellow gold and silver-thin :
*Pierrot and Harlequin*
                    *And Columbine !*

Oh, the people that have seen,
  They forget that it was so!
They, who never stay at home,
  Say, " 'Tis nothing but a show."
— And I keep the passion in :
And I bide ; and I spin.
*Columbine . . . Harlequin*

                    *. . . Pierrot !*

## RETURN

SOLDIER–BOY, soldier-boy,
Now the war is done,
Are you not a happy lad
To see the world at one ?
Home again — home again,
Living, in the sun !

"Oh, the faces smiled on us
While the faces passed ;
And the cannon hailed the flags
Waving from the mast.
It was good, it was good, —
Ah, too good to last.

"Now the streets are still again,
Still enough to fret,
Though the hurts you do not see
May be aching yet,
What we gave, what we won,
Most of you forget.

"For however much I pay
There is more to owe ;
And I must be doing still,
And choose my yes and no !

But friend to me or enemy, —
   Who wears aught to show ?

" Taking orders from myself
   Leaves me many ways ;
And there isn't much to choose
   When a man obeys !
But a bullet keeps its word
   When a kiss betrays."

Soldier-boy, soldier-boy,
   Tell me what you bring
From the wisdom of the war
   Years and nations sing.
" What is death ?   A bitter breath !
   Life's the hardest thing."

## WORDS FOR AN IRISH FOLK-SONG

OH, my day is lone. May every day be fair
to you ! —
Shining like the moon you are, too far to see.
But I ease my heart with singing all my care to
you,
Where I cannot grieve you with the grief in me.

Here I wait and work ; and never catch a gleam
of you,
And you never feel my longing, over-sea.
Ah, but Blessèd Eyes, such comfort's in the dream
of you,
I can stay my heart to earn the joy for you and
me !

## LIGHT   IN   DARK

IT was the twilight made you look
So kindly and so far.
It was the twilight gave your eyes
  A shadow, and a star.

For loveliness is not to keep
  Unto the skies alone ;
And though the glories may be gone,
  The heart will have its own.

Some likeness of a dream is shed
  From all fair things, too far ;
And so your eyes have left to me
  A shadow and a star.

## A SPINNING-SONG

MOTHER, dear, I do not leave
Old love for a new:
This is older far than all,
  If the stars be true.

When I answered to his look,
  A little moon ago,
Ah, that early greeting woke
  All I used to know!

Then I heard the Deep call
  Round about our mirth;
Then I felt the Garden breath,
  Older than the earth.

So we walked together once, —
  Brow and brow as near,
Shining with the dew from off
  Trees that held us dear.

Oh, it is no gypsy-light,
  Bids me forth, to roam! —
But my own star in his eyes,
  Wanting me at home!

## MIRANDA

HOW could I tell, so unaware,
That it was all for you
The suns shed gold upon my hair,
And all the lost leaves shadowed there,
And deeps of far star-lighted air
    Left in my eyes their blue ?
But now I know that I am fair,
        For you !

Oh, never doubt that whatsoe'er
    Of beautiful for you
My mother April lets me wear,
Summer shall make it richer fair
For kindly Frost to see — and spare,
    Till lover's charm renew.
Nay, Earth will heed the little prayer ! —
        For you.

## THE BELOVED

I HAVE no mirror any more,
  Save in belovèd eyes,
Where only I behold myself
    Beautiful, and wise.

Oh, I am wise with all the light
  The waking garden knows;
And I will lift my heart therein,
    Blessed as a Rose.

## GOOD–NIGHT

GOOD–NIGHT, my burden.  Rest you
    there,
    The working hours are over ;
Poor weight, that had to be my care,
    And why, let time discover !
The evening star sheds down on me
    The dearer look than laughter,
At whose clear call I put by all
    Forbids me follow after ; —
Free, free to breathe First-Breath again, the breath
    of all hereafter !

    Good-night, heart's grief : and rest you there,
        Until your own to-morrow.
    Here's only place for that wide air
        More old, more young, than sorrow.
    And though I hear, from far without,
        These caging winds keep revel,
    Oh, yet I must bestow some trust
        Where water seeks her level,
Where wise-heart water seeks and sings, until
    she reach the level.

*God bless this little share of bread,*
*This water from the spring,*
*The wayside boon of rest at noon*
*When we go hungering:*
*And as we shoulder care again,*
*God make us all to sing!*